IMAGES
of America

NEW LONDON

The sidewalks of lower State Street were full of people on this day in the 1870s. The building in the far distance is the old railway station, which burned in 1885, prompting the building of Union Station. (Public Library of New London.)

IMAGES
of America

NEW LONDON

John J. Ruddy

ARCADIA

ISBN 0-7524-0949-2

Published by Arcadia Publishing,
an imprint of the Chalford Publishing Corporation,
One Washington Center, Dover, New Hampshire 03820.
Printed in Great Britain

Library of Congress Cataloging-in-Publication Data applied for

A group of workmen and two small boys posed for this group shot at Bank and State Streets around the turn of the century. In the background are the Soldiers and Sailors Monument and the Neptune Building. (Carol Kimball Collection.)

Contents

The unpaved expanse of the Parade as it looked in the 1870s. At right is the Liberty Pole, a landmark for years before the Soldiers and Sailors Monument was erected in 1896. (Brian McCarthy.)

Introduction

When the camera's infant eyes first beheld New London, the city was in the midst of its greatest days.

The arrival of the first photographers in the mid-nineteenth century coincided with the height of the whaling industry, which gave the city lasting renown. Though most of the early photographs show more streets and people than whaling ships, they reflect nonetheless a place that had every reason to be optimistic about its future.

They also show a city that had a storied past, even then. New London's great calamity, the burning of the town by Benedict Arnold, was still within living memory of the oldest residents. The fire spared more buildings than is generally supposed, and many of them were around long enough to be photographed.

All cities change, and New London was bound to lose some of its ancient places to the march of progress. But unlike many others, the Whaling City was fated to withstand two more landmark-leveling disasters in the twentieth century: one, the 1938 hurricane, was an act of God; the other was a man-made orgy of destruction called Redevelopment.

Thus the value of old photographs increases in proportion to what has been lost, which is a lot. New London was a very different place 150 years ago, both in what it looked like and in what it was all about. Seeing it captured by the camera is as close as we're likely to get to a journey back in time to experience it first-hand.

If New Londoners of today could visit that long-ago place, they would have no trouble finding their way around. The paths of the main streets have changed relatively little since they were laid down in the 1600s. But not much else would be familiar. Most of the buildings and monuments now inseparable from the city's identity were still shadows of the future. Where Union Station now sits as the capstone of the waterfront, there was only a broad view of the Thames River. Where John Winthrop, cast in bronze, gazes over the city he founded, there was only an empty square. Where the Mohican Hotel rises 11 stories to dwarf everything around it, there was a private residence.

New Londoners of those days got their bearings from other landmarks, long vanished, with strange-sounding names like Mount Vernon, Bacon's Hotel, and the

Old Yellow Building.

A time traveller stepping off the Groton ferry at the foot of State Street could take comfort in a few instantly familiar sights. Before him would stretch the vast expanse of the Parade, recognizable even without the Soldiers and Sailors Monument. A giant flagpole, called the Liberty Pole, would stand in its place, but to the left would be, as today, the corner of Bank Street. And up State Street, rising beyond a cluster of trees, the stone spire of the First Congregational Church would anchor the backward-flowing years, unchanged and looking as though it had always been there.

This book encompasses two journeys in time. The first goes from today back to the 1850s, the time of the earliest surviving photographs of New London. The second goes forward from there more than half a century to the days just before World War I, when the last whaler had shipped out and the first submarine was about to arrive.

During those eventful years, New London remained a vital place. Before interstate highways bled cities everywhere of citizens and commerce, they were the focal points of life, and New London was no exception. The city had a booming business center on State Street and factories that churned out everything from textiles to crackers to cotton gins.

It was also, for a time, a fashionable place for the wealthy, who created an exclusive resort community in the south end. Throughout the second half of the nineteenth century, the Pequot Colony was frequented by the cream of society, including actors, diplomats, and presidents.

As a place worth getting to, and blessed by its location halfway between New York and Boston, New London became a transportation hub. A key stop on the mixed rail-and-steamer trips between the two cities, it was also the site of the last missing link in the shoreline rail route, which was filled by the first Thames River bridge in 1889.

Most of all, New London retained its relationship with the sea. The whalers disappeared, but the shipping business remained strong, and the Navy was a frequent visitor before it became a permanent resident.

Even in those heady days, New London seemed ambivalent about the treasures of its past. In 1860, historian Frances Manwaring Caulkins had this to say about the courthouse at the head of State Street: "It is a wooden building, ungraceful, common-place and generally regarded as an unsightly blot, disfiguring the neighborhood where it stands, yet, as a stately relic of a former age, still doing service in this,—it maintains its respectability and is regarded with interest." More than a century later, seized with a fit of collective insanity, New Londoners almost turned their beautiful, Richardson Romanesque train station into rubble.

Today, thankfully, both buildings are still with us and face each other as the anchors of the downtown, holding the length of the city's main street in their mutual gaze. Not having them there has become unthinkable.

Slowly, New London is learning to revere its history. May this book be a part of that long-overdue process.

One

An Early Tour of the City

The Benjamin Brown House on Bank Street, opposite Tilley, was built in 1817 and still stands, but it has undergone a radical change in appearance. The columns and roof over the front porch are gone, and the four first-floor windows were converted into two bow windows when the building was a store. (Courtesy New London County Historical Society.)

In the late 1840s, State Street, later the city's main commercial thoroughfare, was largely residential. Dr. Dyer T. Brainard, a noted physician, poses before 1850 in front of his home opposite Green Street. The Brainard Masonic lodge was named for the doctor. (Public Library of New London.)

The Crocker House was erected on the site of this impressive home on State Street. It was built by Dr. James Lee, who came to New London from Lyme to assist in caring for the victims of the yellow fever outbreak of 1798. Later occupants included Augustus Brandegee, seen here, a prominent judge and legislator. (Public Library of New London.)

This Greek Revival house built in the 1820s and seen here around 1860 was, successively, the home of Robert Coit, Uriah Rogers, and Alfred H. Chappell. It sat at Huntington and Federal Streets, opposite St. James Church, and was torn down in 1932. The site was later occupied by a car dealership. (Courtesy New London County Historical Society.)

Across Union Street from the Brandegee home was the residence of Increase Wilson, who opened New London's first factory, a coffee mill plant, in 1827. The house was torn down in 1896, and the site became home to the post office, and later, Montgomery Ward. Today Southern New England Telephone Co. is located here. (Public Library of New London.)

Charles H. Gay took this panoramic daguerreotype of the New London waterfront from Groton in 1851. Fort Trumbull is visible in the second panel, and the spire of the First Congregational Church rises to the right of the ships in the fourth. Both buildings were brand

Bartlett High School was the city's secondary school for young men before the Bulkeley School opened in 1873. The Class of 1864 included Walter Learned, seated at far right, later a prominent officer of the Savings Bank of New London and a published poet. (Public Library of New London.)

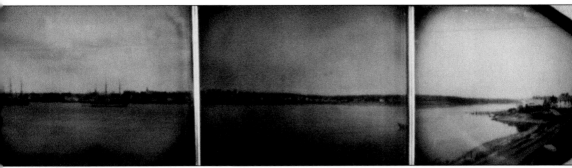

new at the time. No bridge spanned the Thames River until 1889. (The J. Paul Getty Museum, Los Angeles.)

Young ladies of New London attended the appropriately named Young Ladies High School in the days before Williams Memorial Institute. This picture may have been taken in front of a church on Golden Street, where the school moved in 1866. (Public Library of New London.)

The corner of State (right) and Main was called Buttonwood Corner, after this large sycamore or buttonwood tree. Known as the "Charter Oak of New London," it was cut down in 1856, the same year the real Charter Oak, in Hartford, blew down in a storm. In 1781 British sympathizers friendly with Benedict Arnold lived in this house, which was spared when Arnold burned the town. At the time of this photograph it was a grocery run by Charles and James Strickland. (Public Library of New London.)

Other notable trees included the "Four Sisters," a row of elms in front of the General Henry Burbeck House on Main Street near Church. Built in 1735, the house was later occupied by Burbeck, the local military commander in the War of 1812. The elms were named Johanna, Catherine, Sophia, and Sarah, for the daughters of James Baxter, another owner. (Public Library of New London.)

Main Street was lined with stores selling books, boots, jewelry, and hardware around 1880. The big building at right housed the Rogers Ice Co. Behind the horse in the distance is the original building of the Savings Bank of New London. (Courtesy New London County Historical Society.)

Soldiers gather for a patriotic portrait in front of the courthouse on Huntington Street during the Civil War. Soldiers were a common sight in New London during the war, since Fort Trumbull was the mustering point for troops from throughout Connecticut who were preparing to head south to the fighting. (Mystic Seaport Museum.)

Bacon's Hotel on Bank Street appears to have no vacancies in this scene from the 1870s. Dating to the 1830s, when it was one of the city's only hotels, Bacon's did a brisk business from its location near Steamboat Wharf at the foot of Golden Street and was a stopping point for the Colchester stage. Famous guests included statesman Daniel Webster. (Richard Gipstein.)

A third floor was added, the ground floor converted to storefronts, and the whole thing renamed the Bacon House around 1880. On July 10, 1897, the old landmark burned to the ground. Its owner immediately built the Hotel Royal, which still stands on the site. (Courtesy New London County Historical Society.)

Just as celebrated as Bacon's Hotel was the City Hotel on lower State Street, which dated to the 1790s. It was host to President Andrew Jackson in the summer of 1833, and future presidents Martin Van Buren and Abraham Lincoln also were guests. The City Hotel survived two fires

but was destroyed by a third on April 9, 1891. The Cronin Building replaced it the following year. (Public Library of New London.)

After the Second Congregational Church at Huntington and Jay Streets burned in 1868, a new building was planned for Broad and Hempstead Streets. A crowd of five hundred gathered October 29, 1868, to lay the cornerstone. A box placed in the stone contained coins, paper currency, postage stamps, and newspapers of the day, a picture of the old church, two almanacs, sermons, hymns, and official papers. (Public Library of New London.)

By 1870 all the new church was missing was its now-familiar steeple. The new building was dedicated June 1, 1870. The market building at left was later a succession of candy stores, including the long-lived Capitol Candy Shop. (Public Library of New London.)

The Fitch residence stood at Broad and Williams Streets, facing Broad, when this photograph was taken around 1885. A large brick apartment house is now on the site. At far left part of a bandstand is visible in Williams Park. (Public Library of New London.)

The still-unpaved State Street was lined with trees in this view looking toward the Thames River. At left, behind the trees, are the First Congregational Church and City Hall. Commercial activity was then concentrated at the lower end of the street. (Brian McCarthy.)

A longtime landmark was the "Old Yellow Building," located at State and Bradley Streets, on the Parade. Seen here in the 1860s, when it housed a hardware store, Old Yellow was around until 1898, when it was razed to make way for another landmark, the Neptune Building. (Courtesy New London County Historical Society.)

Around 1866 only the spire of the First Congregational Church and the twin spires of the Federal Street Methodist Church rose above the low-lying city in this view from the Starr House on the far side of Winthrop Cove in East New London. (Courtesy New London County Historical Society.)

A pedestrian bridge crossed Winthrop Cove between Main and Winthrop Streets in the 1870s. In the distance is the Starr House, at Crystal Avenue and Front Street. (Public Library of New London.)

The Williams Mansion at State and Huntington Streets was built by Thomas W. Williams, a whaling merchant, in 1831. It is shown here in a photograph taken at State and Meridian looking toward Huntington after being extensively renovated around 1880 by Thomas's son, Charles Augustus Williams. In the 1920s the mansion was razed to make way for what is now the Garde Arts Center. (Public Library of New London.)

Bradley Street, c. 1868, was also known as Widows' Row and was spared from Benedict Arnold's torch. Later known as North Bank Street, it is today an empty and non-descript route called Atlantic Street, which runs between the Day building and the Water Street parking garage. (Brian McCarthy.)

Directly across State Street from the Williams Mansion stood the Stewart House. In 1890 this building was torn down to make way for the Public Library of New London. The building at left was the last surviving house on State Street when it was razed in 1957. The library parking lot is now on the site. (Courtesy New London County Historical Society.)

The Parade at the foot of State Street was a wide-open space for horses and carriages when photographer Edward T. Avery captured it in the early 1870s. The area was so-called because it was once a parade ground for soldiers. At left, on the corner of Bank Street, was the office of the *Daily Star*, a newspaper of the time. (Courtesy New London County Historical Society.)

Bank Street, looking toward State, seems totally alien except for the building behind the meat store sign, the U.S. Custom House, which was built in 1833. The building's architect, Robert Mills, also designed the Washington Monument. (Richard Gipstein.)

A view of Bank Street from the opposite direction doesn't look much more familiar. The sign over the sidewalk at right advertises Steinways and Chickerings, two well-known makers of pianos. (Brian McCarthy.)

The Bishop Lumber Yard was established on the part of Bank Street known as "Long Bridge," an area between Howard Street and the Shaw Mansion that was once a bridge over the waters of Shaw's Cove. John Bishop was one of many landowners who gradually filled in the area during the mid-nineteenth century. (Public Library of New London.)

This view from the Shaw Mansion, looking across Perkins Green, shows that Shaw's Cove reached all the way to Bank Street as late as the 1880s. The house, itself on a square of land reclaimed from the cove, sits about where the Steinman Building later was erected. (Public Library of New London.)

The First Congregational Church is the only familiar sight in this early view of Masonic Street, seen from Main. The building with the flag at left is probably the Nameaug Fire Co., which was located just to the rear of City Hall for years. (Lyman Allyn Art Museum, New London, Conn.)

Federal Street, seen from Broad, once ran all the way to Water Street but now stops at Union. A church is once again the sole surviving landmark, in this case St. James Episcopal. Farther on are the twin spires of the Federal Street Methodist Church, where the rear parking lot of the Radisson Hotel is now. (Brian McCarthy.)

Two

Down to the Sea

A U.S. Navy warship sails in the Thames River during a visit to New London around the turn of the century. The Griswold Hotel, a landmark of Groton's Eastern Point, is visible at right. (New London Landmarks.)

This is believed to be the whaling bark *George Henry* in the Thames River around 1856. One of a fleet of whaling ships in New London, the *George Henry* discovered the British exploration vessel HMS *Resolute* abandoned and icebound west of Greenland in 1855. Capt. James M. Buddington of the *George Henry* sailed the *Resolute* to New London, and it was later returned to Queen Victoria. When the *Resolute* was scrapped in 1880, a desk was fashioned from its timbers and presented to President Rutherford B. Hayes. Today the desk sits in the Oval Office at the White House. As for the *George Henry*, it was crushed in the ice of Hudson Bay in 1863. (Courtesy New London County Historical Society.)

Thomas W. Williams dispatched the first whaling ship from New London in 1819, and the industry grew rapidly. By its peak in 1845, there were 81 vessels homeported in the city under the control of 14 firms. By the Civil War, whaling had passed its peak, but there were still enough ships here to fill up the harbor. (Public Library of New London.)

Part of the crew of the whaling schooner *Era* poses on the ship's deck. Built in Boston in 1847, the *Era* had an eventful career. It brought an Inuit known as John Bull to New London to testify in a court case, and its last voyage in 1892 marked the end of 75 years in the whaling business by the Williams family. (Public Library of New London.)

Mortally wounded by the California gold rush and the Civil War, the whaling industry went into a long, slow decline. But the last whaler did not depart the city until 1910, just six years before the first submarine arrived. This scene is from 1866. (Courtesy New London County Historical Society.)

Three two-masted schooners lie tied up on the bank of the Thames River, with a fourth one nearby, around the turn of the century. Between the masts of the second ship from the right, the Groton Monument is visible on the opposite shore. (Courtesy New London County Historical Society.)

In 1860 whaling magnate Sebastian Lawrence bought and refitted the schooner *Charles Colgate*, named for a New York soap manufacturer. Originally a New York-Charleston packet, the *Colgate* made 11 successful voyages for Lawrence's firm. Here it is docked at Lawrence Wharf behind Bank Street. (Public Library of New London.)

Lawrence retired the *Charles Colgate* in 1884 and later dreamed of refitting it as a relic of the whaling days. But in 1897 the ship sank at the wharf, and Lawrence had it towed to the muddy flats of Winthrop Cove, near his home. There it sat for decades, a symbol of a lost era, until it slowly rotted away. (Courtesy New London County Historical Society.)

Local men who had served at least two years at sea, many on whaling voyages, organized the Jibboom Club No. 1 in 1891 and assembled a whaling museum at the club's headquarters at Bank and Golden Streets. There were once as many as three hundred members. The club

Each year on Washington's birthday, the Jibboom Club held a parade through town, followed by a dinner and dance. This photograph was taken during the 1907 celebration. (Public Library of New London.)

endured until 1959, when the 10 surviving members' dues could no longer pay the rent. (Public Library of New London.)

The coasting schooner *Reindeer* sails down the Thames river, approaching Fort Trumbull, at left. Two other ships are visible at their moorings north of the fort. (Mystic Seaport Museum.)

Navy ships frequently visited New London, even before the future Naval Submarine Base in Groton was established as a coaling station in 1868. The sailing frigate USS *Sabine* was stationed here from the end of the Civil War until 1868. The *Sabine* was a training ship for Navy apprentices and landsmen. (Public Library of New London.)

Looking down State Street from Main, the USS *Sabine* is visible in the river, just to the left of the old railroad station. The frigate was a familiar sight during its three-year assignment here. (William Peterson Collection.)

The sloop of war USS *Jamestown* had a long, eventful career that included bringing food to famine-stricken Ireland. In 1882, it was fitted out as an apprentice training ship and was later photographed on a visit to New London. The first bridge over the Thames River can be seen in the background. (Public Library of New London.)

Like the Jamestown, the USS *St. Mary's* was a sloop of war that later became a training ship. It was operated by the Public Marine School in New York when it visited New London around the turn of the century. Groton's Eastern Point is at left. (Connecticut State Library.)

Though not known as a fishing port, New London sometimes welcomed fishing vessels like this smack from about 1880. John Ashcroft, the captain, is at far right. (Courtesy New London County Historical Society.)

Even after whaling died out, shipping activity remained heavy as New London maintained its longtime link with the sea. Barges line the Thames in this turn-of-the-century view. In the left foreground is the rear of the Crocker House at Union and Golden Streets. (*The Day.*)

In 1760 a lottery was organized to build a lighthouse at the entrance to New London Harbor. It was the first lighthouse on the Connecticut coast. In 1801 the old lighthouse was replaced by this 89-foot sandstone structure called New London Harbor Light. It is seen here in the 1880s, during the brief life of Osprey Beach. (Public Library of New London.)

In 1908–1909 a second lighthouse was built on Southwest Ledge, a major hazard to navigation at the harbor entrance. Seen here under construction, New London Ledge Light is a three-story red brick building in the French Second Empire style. (Connecticut State Library.)

Employees of Thames Towboat Co. stand alongside one of the company's tugs moored in the Thames around 1910. The company, which originated in Norwich and moved to New London in 1879, towed all along the Atlantic seaboard. (Public Library of New London.)

The sea also provided recreation, as it does today. The Rambler Boat Club was one of many that once existed along the coast. This photograph was probably taken in the summer of 1909, just after construction of the marine cradle in the foreground. State Pier was later erected from this spot. (Lyman Allyn Art Museum, New London, Conn.)

Three
Business and Industry

C.B. Ware & Co. sold clothing and furnishing goods from this store on lower State Street, near the Parade. Upstairs was Edward T. Avery's photograph gallery, which produced this picture in the 1870s. (Courtesy New London County Historical Society.)

Frederick Stein's book and stationery store was one of the many businesses along State Street when most anything one needed was available there. According to his sign, Stein carried school books and even spectacles for reading them. (William Peterson Collection.)

Thomas Ealahan Sr. stands in front of the saloon he operated on John Street around the turn of the century. John Street was off Main and is now part of Atlantic Street. (Marjorie Ealahan Heap.)

The wagon of the W.R. Perry Ice Co. was a common sight in the days before refrigerators. This photograph was taken on Broad Street around 1912. The man at right is Lafayette G. Sharp. (Public Library of New London.)

An earlier ice business was that of the Rogers Brothers, which dated to 1834 and lasted until 1899. George P. Rogers is shown here weighing a block of ice in front of the store on State Street. The ice was cut from Rock Reservoir off Bloomingdale Road in Waterford. The Mariners Savings Bank later occupied the building, which was located next to the old post office. (Public Library of New London.)

W.S. Chappell stands in front of his grocery store on State Street at Green in the early 1890s. Behind and to Chappell's left is Charles Daboll. At right the man wearing the sandwich board is advertising a sale at Barrows the Shoeman on Bank Street. (Public Library of New London.)

After President James A. Garfield was assassinated, Chappell, along with probably many businessmen throughout the country, decorated his display window to mourn the slain leader. Garfield was shot by a disappointed office seeker on July 2, 1881, and died two months later. (Public Library of New London.)

John Denison's carpenter shop was behind Bank Street along the railroad tracks. A sign proclaims that saws can be filed and set, and other signs advertise the Lawrence Opera House and Brainerd & Armstrong, a New London silk factory. The brick building at left is the Whaling Bank. Note the birdhouse on a pole above the shop. (Public Library of New London.)

The Pequot Steam Laundry at 40 Pequot Avenue was established in 1876. The proprietor was Charles L. Ockford, later chief of the Ockford Hose Co. Ockford also co-owned and managed Osprey Beach in the 1880s. (Public Library of New London.)

W.P. Benjamin & Co., a women's clothing store on lower State Street, was established in 1833 and was still in business around the turn of the century. As employees pose beneath two women's coats, a sign in the window advertises "fur trimmings & muffs at cost." (Public Library of New London.)

Inside W.P. Benjamin & Co., merchandise lined both walls of the narrow store. Carpets, draperies, and dry goods were sold here as well as garments. Mourning dresses were a specialty. The sign at center reads, "Peerless Patterns." (Public Library of New London.)

Union Bank was the first bank in Connecticut when it was established in 1792. Only five other banks then existed in the country. This building was erected on lower State Street in 1818. Though its name changed several times, the bank retained its identity until 1963, when it merged into the Connecticut Bank and Trust Co. (Lyman Allyn Art Museum, New London, Conn.)

In 1827 a new institution, the Savings Bank of New London, opened. The bank moved into its home on Main Street in 1852. This small brick box was widened and renovated considerably around the turn of the century and today looks nothing like its former self. The bank finally closed after more than 150 years of operation. (Citizens Bank.)

Employees of the Arnold Rudd Co. line up for a rather severe portrait in front of the store on Bank Street. Rudd erected the building in 1886. Along with flour and sugar, he sold items just as essential in the pre-automobile era: hay and straw for horses. At left is the Troy Steam Laundry. (Courtesy New London County Historical Society.)

Another essential commodity was horseshoes. J.A. Glasbrenner ran one of several business in New London that met the demand. This building was once the home of the W.B. Thomas Hose Co. and was located on Williams Street, around the corner from Huntington. The streets once met where Interstate 95 now runs. (Courtesy New London County Historical Society.)

Nichols & Harris was a wholesale druggist that did business in New London for more than 35 years, with shops on Main and State Streets. This photograph was taken on March 31, 1896. (Courtesy New London County Historical Society.)

Main and Williams Streets, the area known as Hodges Square, was the site of this store around 1898. The proprietor was Charles J. Hewitt (center), who was later the city's street commissioner. At left is Charles Benham, and the man at right is identified only as "a man named Short."

A.B. Currier, an auctioneer, occupied this familiar stone building on Bank Street around 1873. Among the later occupants were Darrow and Comstock. In recent years the building has been the home of Roberts, which sells stereo equipment. (Courtesy New London County Historical Society.)

In the same building as Currier, Walter S. Calvert sold pictures, frames, window shades, and looking glasses in the 1870s. The door to the shop was at the far left of the building. (Public Library of New London.)

Peterson's, a well-known confectionery and ice cream parlor on State Street, was established around 1900 by Socrates Patterson and his nephew, Stavros Peterson, both Greek immigrants. It was noted for its home-made ice cream. (Carol Kimball Collection.)

The Day, founded in 1881, was the only one of New London's many newspapers to survive. Originally located in the building where Currier had operated, the paper had several homes before settling into its present location in 1907. This group of employees gathered for a portrait in the 1880s.

C.D. Boss and Son on Water Street had roots dating back to before the Revolution, when it began as a bakery. By stocking whaling ships, the company grew into a giant manufacturer of crackers and biscuits and had a national reputation. Its signature product was the Lunch Milk Biscuit, varieties of which are still made. (Courtesy New London County Historical Society.)

New London was once a center of cotton gin manufacturing. The Brown Cotton Gin Co. (shown here) was on Pequot Avenue, and the Albertson and Douglass Machine Company was on Main Street. The two held a sizable share of the market. The building used by Brown later housed companies that made printing presses, machine tools, and linoleum. (Lyman Allyn Art Museum, New London, Conn.)

The women of the chenille department stand in front of their looms at the Brainerd and Armstrong Co., a textile manufacturer and one of the city's major employers with 1,500 workers. Founded after the Civil War, the company started off making and selling spool silks in rented quarters on the waterfront. (Public Library of New London.)

By 1885 Brainerd and Armstrong had grown large enough for its own building, so it erected this massive structure at Church and Union Streets, the present site of the parking garage on Governor Winthrop Boulevard. The company, which eventually opened two other plants in the city and one in Norwich, operated well into the twentieth century. (Courtesy New London County Historical Society.)

Employees of the D.E. Whiton Machine Co. work among a tangle of machinery in February 1906. Whiton made centering machines, lathe and drill chucks, and gear-cutting machines at its factory on Howard Street. The machine tools were widely used in the United States and England. (Museum of Connecticut History.)

The site of New London's first factory, the Wilson Manufacturing Co. at Washington and Methodist Streets, was later used by the Palmer Brothers Co., which made quilts here and at several locations in Montville. This aerial view is from the turn of the century. Southern New England Telephone Co. now occupies the site. (Carol Kimball Collection.)

Four

Transportation Center

The *City of New York* was one of many steamboats that linked New London and New York. Built in 1862, the 300-foot vessel was made of white oak. Behind it at left may be its sister ship, the *City of Boston*. New London enjoyed steamboat service from 1840 to 1934. (Public Library of New London.)

Bank Street, here passing the building that later housed Ye Olde Tavern, was part of the southerly route of the Boston Post Road, the old mail route between Boston and New York. Throughout the first half of the nineteenth century, this route was operated as a commercial toll road, the New London and Lyme Turnpike, between the city and the Connecticut River. (Brian McCarthy.)

Roadside taverns were a feature of the old turnpikes, and Belcher Tavern, on Hempstead Street at Broad, was the last stopping place in town on the Hartford and New London Turnpike. It included a bowling alley, and the favored drink was "flip"—cider mixed with brandy or rum, baking soda, and a baked crab apple. (Lyman Allyn Art Museum, New London, Conn.)

Ferries had plied the Thames River between New London and Groton since sailboats were used in the 1600s. A ferry powered by four horses on a treadmill was used from 1821 to 1849, followed by steam-powered vessels such as the *Mohegan*, seen here in 1862. Avery Chester Perkins, the captain, is in the pilot house. The *Mohegan* made two trips an hour between 6 a.m. and 9 p.m. (Public Library of New London.)

There were both passenger ferries, such as the *Mohegan*, and boats to shuttle railroad cars across the unbridged Thames. A train is shown here backing onto a railroad ferry behind Bank Street before 1889, when the first railroad bridge opened. The tall building at rear is the Metropolitan Hotel, and the two-chimneyed structure to the left is the Whaling Bank. (Public Library of New London.)

The Ontalaunee was an early locomotive used on the railroad first known as the New London, Willimantic & Palmer, and later as the New London Northern. The first train trip out of the city took place November 15, 1849. (Courtesy New London County Historical Society.)

Train travel had its perils. On the morning of November 1, 1878, the boiler of the Stafford, a locomotive of the New London Northern Railroad, exploded at the depot at the foot of State Street. Thirty-year-old Bradford C. Rand, a conductor standing on the platform, was killed by flying debris. (Public Library of New London.)

The locomotive Robert Coit emerges from the roundhouse at the foot of Fourth Street in East New London, which was built in the 1870s for the New London Northern Railroad. The site also included repair shops. (Public Library of New London.)

Engineers, firemen, and conductors of the New London Northern Railroad stand before the brick engine house on Fourth Street in East New London in the 1880s. The tall, bearded man at rear is Master Mechanic I.W. Dow. (Public Library of New London.)

By the late 1880s, the shoreline rail route between Boston and New York still had one gap: a bridge across the Thames. Surveys for a bridge had been made as early as 1859, but the job was long considered impossible, and construction did not begin until 1888. This photograph was taken looking south (New London is at right). (Connecticut State Library.)

By the fall of 1889 the bridge was complete, and at 1,423 feet, it was the longest double-track drawbridge in the world. At the opening ceremony on October 10, the railroad ferry *Groton* passed through the open draw, symbolizing the end of one era and the beginning of another. In the foreground is the Bragaw shipyard. (Public Library of New London.)

But ferries, such as the *Col. Ledyard*, were still needed for everyday travel to and from Groton. Even after a new railroad bridge was built during World War I and the old bridge given over to passenger use, ferries remained by popular demand. Service was not discontinued until 1929. (Lyman Allyn Art Museum, New London, Conn.)

Plans for a street railway had been kicking around for several years before the streets were finally dug up and tracks laid in the summer of 1892. This was Bank Street near the Shaw Mansion. The Putnam Furniture Manufacturing Co. is at right. (Public Library of New London.)

Enthusiastic riders mobbed the trolleys on the first day of service in November 1892. This photograph was taken by William H. Bishop on Bank Street near Montauk Avenue, then known as the Boulevard. The buildings in the background, including Lennen's kindling wood plant (at right) and Polo Rogers' saloon, were later removed and the area converted into Garibaldi Park.

An empty Car 13 turns turns from Huntington Street onto State in the winter of 1893. The word "Boulevard," on the side of the car, was the original name of Montauk Avenue, which had just been constructed. At right is the Williams Mansion, now the site of the Garde Arts Center. (Courtesy New London County Historical Society.)

Three cars travel near the Parade at the foot of State Street on March 31, 1896. The Parade served as the point of origination for all trolley routes throughout the city. At far left is the corner of State and Main Streets. Trolleys ran in New London until 1932. (Courtesy New London County Historical Society.)

Sprinkler trolleys kept the streets free of dust arising from the macadam roads and were used until about 1915. Most of the car consisted of a tank, and water was sprayed from two nozzles in front. Sand was sprinkled from the rear to keep the tracks from getting slippery. Robert Durkee (left) and Lou Roath ran this sprinkler on Truman Street near Blackhall.

The city's street department maintained a more old-fashioned conveyance for keeping the streets clean, but it served the same purpose, with the added advantage of being able to travel on roads the track-bound sprinkler trolleys could not reach. (Carol Kimball Collection.)

Automobiles were still a novelty when this photograph was taken around 1908. When jeweler Henry F. Macomber bought a little steam Oldsmobile in October 1900, he became the first car owner in New London. Amazed crowds followed him everywhere and even watched him flirt with disaster as he skidded across the frozen surface of Lake Brandegee. (Public Library of New London.)

The Parade, as it is today, was a transportation center when this scene was captured in 1883. The steamboat *City of Worcester* departs on an excursion to Newport, RI, while the passenger ferry *Uncas* sits docked in front of it. At right is the railroad ferry *Groton*. The building at far right is the old railway station. (Lyman Allyn Art Museum, New London, Conn.)

Since New London was a major stop on the steamboat lines, it was only appropriate that a boat bear the city's name. The *City of New London* was built in New York in 1863 and was owned by the Norwich and New York Line. (Connecticut Historical Society, Hartford, Conn.)

The *City of New London*'s career came to a tragic end on November 22, 1871, when it caught fire in the Thames River, 9 miles north of the city. The crew extinguished the flames and proceeded toward Norwich, but near Poquetanuck Cove the fire rekindled in some cotton on deck and spread out of control. Seventeen people were killed. (Carol Kimball Collection.)

The 235-foot steamer *City of Lawrence* went into service in 1867 and served on the Norwich-to-New York route for years. Later it was a Block Island excursion boat. On the morning of July 2, 1907, in a dense fog, the *Lawrence* struck Black Rock in the mouth of New London Harbor and was a total loss. (Connecticut State Library.)

It was standing room only on the steamer *Richard Peck* as it sailed the Thames River, providing a perfect view of the Yale-Harvard Regatta around the turn of the century. The *Peck*, known as the "Queen of the Sound," usually brought New Haven-area people to New London for the race. (Connecticut State Library.)

The steamer *City of Worcester* of the Norwich Line began service between New York and New London in 1881. It was the first iron-hulled passenger steamer on Long Island Sound and the second with electric lights. The *City of Worcester* survived three groundings and was in service until 1914. (Public Library of New London.)

The officers of the steamer *City of Lowell* sat for a portrait on December 13, 1912. Known as "The Greyhound of the Sound," the *Lowell* was among the most luxurious of the fleet of steamers owned by the Norwich Line, an arm of the Norwich and Worcester Railroad. (Public Library of New London.)

Five

The South End

The Duck Pond at Ocean Beach was located where the miniature golf course is today. The building at center is Wordell's Pavilion, a shore dinner hall, and at left is a trolley platform. (Public Library of New London.)

The southern end of the city was once a fashionable resort for the wealthy known as the Pequot Colony or simply "the Pequot." One of the community's focal points was the Pequot House at Glenwood and Pequot Avenues. It was built in 1852 and managed for 20 years by Henry Scudder Crocker, for whom the Crocker House was later named. (New London Landmarks.)

When the Pequot House burned on May 7, 1908, arson was suspected but never proved. The colony's days as a resort for the wealthy were already numbered, and the fire hastened the end. Prohibition and the stock market crash in 1929 finished it off. (Carol Kimball Collection.)

The Pequot Casino Association, an exclusive club of colony residents, formed in 1890 and erected this building, the Pequot Casino, in 1894. Not a casino in the modern sense, it was a social club for members of the association. At right is New London Harbor Light. (Connecticut State Library.)

The Pequot Casino building has survived four major fires, including this most drastic one in 1908. Each blaze resulted in a radical change in the building's appearance. Today it is two private residences joined by a common courtyard. (New London Landmarks.)

Members of the leisure class settle in along the bank of the Thames River to watch the Yale-Harvard Regatta in the summer of 1898. The photograph was taken by E.H. Newbury. (Mystic Seaport Museum.)

Among the wealthy residents of New London's south end were Alfred Mitchell and his wife, Annie Tiffany Mitchell, daughter of the founder of the Tiffany jewelry empire. After their deaths, their home and grounds became the site of New London Junior College, later renamed Mitchell College. (Lyman Allyn Art Museum, New London, Conn.)

Residents and guests at the Pequot Colony in its heyday included diplomats, two presidents, a chief justice of the Supreme Court, and Shakespearean actor Richard Mansfield. This view of colony residences is along Pequot Avenue near Glenwood. (Public Library of New London.)

Col. Augustus C. Tyler, who commanded the 3rd Regiment, Connecticut Volunteers Infantry in the Spanish-American War, lived in this home called "The Elm" on Pequot Avenue, just south of Gardner. It was the scene of many parties for the New York Yacht Club cruise and the Yale-Harvard Regatta, and later became Home Memorial Hospital, which burned in 1944. (Public Library of New London.)

The south end was more than an exclusive neighborhood. To most, it was where the beaches were. Joseph and Fred Bates offered horse-drawn bus service to the Pequot Colony and Osprey Beach in the 1880s. This photograph was taken outside the Wilson Manufacturing Co. at Washington and Methodist Streets. William Wilson is in the doorway, and Ross Burrows is the driver.

A rival bus service was operated by Joseph A. Burr, who stands in the middle foreground alongside his fleet outside City Hall. The ride from downtown to the beach took about an hour, and the fare was 10¢.

In the days before Ocean Beach, New London had, briefly, a privately run seaside resort called Osprey Beach. Located along the Thames just south of New London Harbor Light, Osprey opened in 1881 and featured a dancing pavilion, bowling alleys, and bathhouses. This view is from the long pier where steamers docked. (Public Library of New London.)

A meal at the huge shore dinner hall cost $1, and steamed clams were in particular demand. A network of steam-heated pipes was built, covered with seaweed, and used for clambakes. (Public Library of New London.)

A man identified as "Capt. Lamphere" paddles in a tub race at Osprey Beach in 1884. That year, the operators of the beach, Ockford and Jerome, decided they could not turn a profit, and the beach closed forever. A group from the Pequot Colony bought the land and wiped out every last trace of the resort. (Hempsted Houses.)

Attention shifted to what was then called White Sands Beach, an undeveloped tract south of Osprey Beach. The city paid $25,000 for the property, which became known as Ocean Beach, and under the direction of former Gov. Thomas Waller, cottages soon sprang up. This scene from about 1900 shows an early boardwalk. (Courtesy New London County Historical Society.)

Waders mug for the camera around the turn of the century at Ocean Beach. Women and even men wore lots more to go in the water back then. At the rear is The Pier, a covered structure where steamers docked, and at left is a bandstand. (Public Library of New London.)

An early ski boarder churns up the waters off Ocean Beach in this scene captured by New London photographer Everett Scholfield. (Mystic Seaport Museum.)

As development increased, the Ocean Beach community was soon large enough to warrant its own police department. The officer in charge, Wilbur F. Lewis, is at center. (Public Library of New London.)

This view of the Ocean Beach waterfront was taken from the end of The Pier, where small steamers docked regularly to deliver and pick up beachgoers. The flag at right is flying from

Like Osprey Beach before it, Ocean Beach had a shore dinner hall, Wordell's Pavilion, located behind the present-day miniature golf course. Cooks and other employees of Wordell's, and of Wilkinson's Bath Houses, sat for this portrait early in the century. (Alma Wies.)

Wordell's, the shore dinner hall. All of these buildings were destroyed in the hurricane of 1938. (Alma Wies.)

Ocean Beach Day, an annual day of games and festivities at the beach, had people out in their Sunday finest as a steamer docks at The Pier. (Connecticut State Library.)

Runners take off at the starting gun during a foot race, one of the events of Ocean Beach Day. (Connecticut State Library.)

Six

The Landmarks

The post office at State and Union Streets is a landmark that did not survive the test of time. Built in 1897 on the site of the Increase Wilson house, it was replaced by a Montgomery Ward store in 1936. At right is the Mariners Savings Bank, a longtime financial institution. (Public Library of New London.)

The Joshua Hempsted House on Hempstead Street holds the distinction of being New London's oldest surviving house. Built in 1678, it was occupied by nine generations of Hempsteds until 1937, and may have been a safe haven on the Underground Railroad. (Connecticut State Library.)

Nearby, at Jay and Hempstead Streets, stands the Nathaniel Hempsted House, which for unknown reasons is often called the Huguenot House. Built in 1758–59, it was once waterfront property before Bream Cove, where Reed Street is, silted up and was filled in. (Public Library of New London.)

The Shaw Mansion has changed little since the 1870s. This stone house on Blinman Street was built in 1756 for Capt. Nathaniel Shaw, a wealthy merchant. Prominent guests included George Washington and the Marquis de Lafayette. Since 1907 the mansion has been the home of the New London County Historical Society. (Brian McCarthy.)

Huntington Street, seen from Broad, was lined with trees around 1885, obscuring the view of one of the city's architectural gems, Whale Oil Row. These four Greek Revival houses were designed in 1830 by Ezra Chappell. The second building from the right, not part of the row, is now the Byles funeral home. (Lyman Allyn Art Museum, New London, Conn.)

The Nathan Hale Schoolhouse had already been moved once before the turn of the century. When the famous patriot taught there in 1774–75 it stood at State and Union Streets, where the Crocker House is, and was called Union Schoolhouse. It was later moved down Union Street, across from Golden, and turned into a residence. (Courtesy New London County Historical Society.)

The building was bought by the Sons of the American Revolution, restored, and moved to Ye Antientest Buriall Ground in 1901. Thus began the schoolhouse's long, strange journey around New London. In 1966 it was moved to Ye Olde Town Mill; in 1975, to Union Street next to City Hall; and in 1988, next to the Soldiers and Sailors Monument. (Courtesy New London County Historical Society.)

Once Ye Antientest Buriall Ground filled in 1793, the Second Burial Ground was opened at Broad and Hempstead Streets. At the instigation of Mayor Charles Augustus Williams, the bodies were removed in 1885 and 1886, and the grounds turned into Williams Memorial Park. This scene is from 1874. (William Peterson Collection.)

When the Second Burial Ground filled, the Third was opened in 1835 at Williams Street and Lincoln Avenue. It, too, was cleared of its bodies, except for some smallpox and yellow fever victims, in 1890, to make way for Nathan Hale Grammar School. (Connecticut State Library.)

By 1850 the city was again short of burial space. A private association formed, purchased a tract off Broad Street called "The Cedars," and named it Cedar Grove Cemetery. Beautifully landscaped and away from the city, Cedar Grove typified the rural cemetery movement of the mid-nineteenth century, which was begun to check the spread of disease. (William Peterson Collection.)

The first Fort Trumbull was built during the Revolution and fell to Benedict Arnold's invading troops. It was rebuilt in 1812, then leveled in 1839 to make way for this magnificent edifice of Millstone granite. During the Civil War the fort was the mustering point for all Connecticut troops. This is how it appeared in 1907, three years before it became the first U.S. Coast Guard Academy. (Courtesy New London County Historical Society.)

The Crocker House opened in 1873 and was part of a new generation of New London hotels that replaced the aging eighteenth-century taverns. Built on the site of the Augustus Brandegee home, it was operated by Henry Scudder Crocker, who also ran the Pequot House in the south end. The top floor later was destroyed in a fire. (Public Library of New London.)

After the old railway station burned in 1885, renowned architect Henry Hobson Richardson designed the Romanesque building called Union Station, which opened in 1887 on the Parade and served all three railroads that ran through the city. (Public Library of New London.)

City Hall at State and Union Streets was built in 1856 and was once a much smaller building. The stone arches on either side of the staircase are still as they were, but the rest of the original brownstone structure is barely recognizable. (Public Library of New London.)

In 1912 City Hall was gutted and turned into virtually a new building. A crowd gathers to lay the cornerstone near the shell of the old structure. The tower at right is that of the Nameaug Fire Company on Masonic Street, and the house in the background stood on the site of the post office, which was built in 1934. (Public Library of New London.)

Whaling merchant Henry P. Haven left $65,000 in his will for charitable purposes, and his executors settled on the gift of a public library. The building was made of Milford granite with brownstone trim, a design in the spirit of Henry Hobson Richardson, the architect of Union Station. (Courtesy New London County Historical Society.)

The interior paneling and woodwork of the original library building is of golden oak. It opened to the public on July 6, 1891, with the original collection supplied by Anna Haven Perkins, Henry P. Haven's daughter. (Public Library of New London.)

In December 1895 publisher Frank A. Munsey electrified New London with the news that he would move his operations to New London to publish *Munsey's Magazine*. The property of Morris W. Bacon at State and Meridian Streets was purchased for $30,000, and work began immediately on a new building. (Public Library of New London.)

The eight-story building, the city's tallest, was completed the following year, but almost immediately, labor troubles forced Munsey to abandon his plans and move to New York. The Munsey Building became the Mohican Hotel, which included a department store. Three floors were later added, including the famous Roof Garden. (Connecticut State Library.)

New London got another enduring landmark in 1895. Sebastian D. Lawrence, a member of a prominent whaling family, announced the gift of a monument to honor the city's soldiers and sailors. Construction began immediately on the Parade, the site of the city's first fort. The monument cost $20,000 and was made of Westerly granite. (Courtesy New London County Historical Society.)

A huge crowd gathered to dedicate the Soldiers and Sailors Monument on May 6, 1896, the 250th anniversary of the founding of New London. An older landmark, the Liberty Pole, is at right. Barely a month later, it was moved to the other end of State Street and installed in front of the courthouse. (Courtesy New London County Historical Society.)

The same day, the cornerstone was laid for a statue of John Winthrop the Younger, who founded New London in 1646. Unfortunately, funding was delayed and the statue, sculpted by Norwich native Bela L. Pratt, was not completed for nearly a decade. Workers are shown here placing the statue on its pedestal shortly before its dedication in 1905. (Courtesy New London County Historical Society.)

A boulder was decided on as the appropriate pedestal, and a perfect specimen was found on the farm of John T. Hicks in Waterford. But moving the 20-ton rock wasn't easy. It was placed on a flat car and hauled by horses on portable railroad tracks over two weeks in March 1905. A trolley finished the job overnight once the street railway was reached. (Courtesy New London County Historical Society.)

Ye Olde Town Mill (left) was established in 1650 to grind corn for the town, and John Winthrop, the founder, was granted exclusive rights. Destroyed in the burning of New London, the mill was rebuilt in 1800. At right is the Winthrop House, built by John Still Winthrop, a great-grandson of the founder, around 1750. (*The Day.*)

The Winthrop House was torn down and replaced by Winthrop School in 1893. This building eventually disappeared as well, and the site is now occupied by the mill and footings of the Gold Star Memorial Bridge. (Connecticut State Library.)

The courthouse at the head of State Street was erected in 1784. Originally it sat in the middle of Huntington Street and was later moved back. British officers attended a peace ball there when the War of 1812 ended. The courthouse is decked out here on April 19, 1911, for a reunion of Civil War veterans. (Connecticut State Library.)

A granite monument to New London's firefighters, another gift of Sebastian Lawrence, was sculpted in the likeness of Frederick L. Allen, a mayor, state legislator, and fire chief. Dedicated in front of the courthouse on July 4, 1898, it was later moved to Riverside Park, then to the fire station at Broad Street and Connecticut Avenue. (Connecticut State Library.)

94

Seven
From Day to Day

Patriotic ceremonies were a fact of life around the turn of the century. This crowd gathered in 1901 to mark the rededication of the Nathan Hale Schoolhouse in Ye Antientest Buriall Ground. In the background is Bulkeley School, the city's high school for boys. (Courtesy New London County Historical Society.)

During the Civil War, life went on despite the terrible news from the battlefields. New Londoners were cheered around 1863 by the arrival of a circus, complete with the traditional parade before the performance. (Courtesy New London County Historical Society.)

State Street traffic comes to a halt as everyone watches a man walk a tightrope over the street, near Main, in the 1870s. The man can be seen between the trees on either side of the street and is holding a long stick for balance. (Lyman Allyn Art Museum, New London, Conn.)

During the presidential campaign of 1868, New London Republicans organized as the "Boys in Blue" to promote the candidacy of Civil War hero Ulysses S. Grant. Torchlight parades and rallies were held to drum up support. Grant won and served two terms. At this rally on the Parade, a sign hung over the street (though appearing backwards) reads, "For President U.S. Grant. For Vice President Schuyler Colfax. 'Let Us Have Peace.' " (Public Library of New London.)

The bobsled "Double Ripper" carries a group of friends celebrating winter down Huntington Street, opposite where the library now stands, around 1881. (Public Library of New London.)

The Nameaug Fire Company, one of the city's many volunteer departments, was organized in 1850 by Frederick L. Allen, and in 1854 it established headquarters on Masonic Street behind City Hall. (Public Library of New London.)

On the 250th anniversary of New London's founding, May 6, 1896, festivities included the dedication of the Soldiers and Sailors Monument, the laying of a cornerstone for the statue of John Winthrop, and an enormous parade. (Courtesy New London County Historical Society.)

Another monument erected for the occasion was this commemorative arch over Huntington Street. The dates 1646 and 1896 appear on both pillars, and a flag-bedecked portrait of Winthrop is at center. The Greek Revival houses of Whale Oil Row can be seen at right. (Courtesy New London County Historical Society.)

Leon Washburn's circus parades down State Street on June 24, 1908. It was always an event when the circus came to town, but even more so here since it was also the eve of the Yale-Harvard Regatta. The day before, as the circus paraded in Niantic, a fruit peddler's horse was scared by the elephants, collapsed, and died. (Public Library of New London.)

Yale's varsity crew team reaches the finish line in the annual Yale-Harvard Regatta, a fixture on the Thames River since 1878. Thousands of spectators lined both banks or came in from out of town by steamer. This photograph was taken from under the old bridge over the Thames, looking toward New London. (Public Library of New London.)

On September 6, 1899, New London and Groton commemorated the Battle of Groton Heights and the burning of New London. In the morning, ceremonies were held at Fort Griswold, and in the afternoon, speeches were made in Ye Antientest Buriall Ground. The speaker's platform was erected on the spot where Benedict Arnold watched the destruction of the town. (Courtesy New London County Historical Society.)

Members of the Palestine Commandery No. 6 Knights Templar pose in full regalia around 1900 on the steps of the Masonic temple at Green and Starr Streets. The building, known as the Brainard Lodge, was home to the Masons for a century. (Public Library of New London.)

Bulkeley School for boys opened in 1873, replacing the old Bartlett High School. Just before the turn of the century Bulkeley produced this lean, stockinged baseball team, which won the state championship. (Public Library of New London.)

Baseball wasn't just for schoolboys. This motley crew of physicians faced off against a team of lawyers on July 13, 1900. A crowd of eight hundred watched the doctors give the lawyers a dose of defeat by a score of 11-10. The man with the gun was an umpire authorized to shoot any player who interfered with him. Base stealers were subject to prosecution. (Public Library of New London.)

The "O'Connells of New London," an amateur football team, were the undefeated New England champions in 1909. Backed by Jack O'Connell, a local politician, the all-Irish team practiced on a baseball field and defeated a team from Worcester, MA, for the title. (*The Day.*)

The newer sport of basketball also occupied the idle hours of New Londoners around the turn of the century. These players stand in front of the net at the YMCA gymnasium on State Street. (Courtesy New London County Historical Society.)

Children participate in a May Pole celebration in Williams Memorial Park at Broad and Hempstead Streets in 1911. The Hempstead Family Association pioneered a playground movement for local children that was eventually taken over by the City. (Courtesy New London County Historical Society.)

This is another view of children's festivities in Williams Memorial Park, the former Second Burial Ground, in the early twentieth century. At left is a stone obelisk honoring New London's Civil War veterans, erected by the state in 1898. (Courtesy New London County Historical Society.)

The New London Playground Committee circulated this shot of a group of city children on a postcard in 1911. The committee was appealing to the public for $700 in support of its plans to open three playgrounds and buy new equipment. (Carol Kimball Collection.)

Members of the Connecticut National Guard stand in formation outside the armory at Coit and Washington Streets around 1908. The commander of the unit was Ernest E. Rogers, later a mayor of New London and lieutenant governor of Connecticut. (Courtesy New London County Historical Society.)

Coit Street School was erected in 1858 and is seen here around 1894. St. Mary's Church is in the background. In 1913 the school was renamed Jennings School to honor Charles B. Jennings, who had run the Town Grammar School in the nineteenth century, and his son, Charles B. Jennings Jr., the city's first superintendent of schools. (Courtesy New London County Historical Society.)

The faculty of Coit Street School, all women, sat for this portrait around 1895. (Courtesy New London County Historical Society.)

The boys and girls of Miss Mary Dugan's class at Coit Street School gathered for a class picture in 1897. With 60 students, the class was more than double the average size of a grade school class today. (Courtesy New London County Historical Society.)

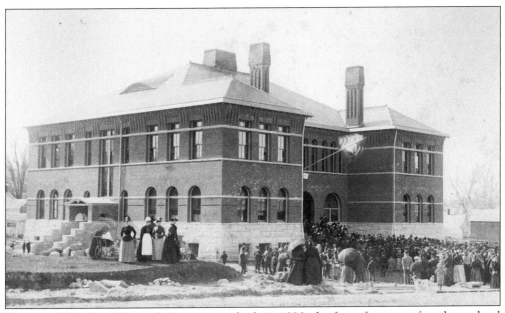

Nameaug School on Montauk Avenue was built in 1890, the first of a wave of modern school buildings erected to replace ancient wooden structures that had outlived their usefulness. The usual crowd of dignitaries and citizens gathered to dedicate the new school. (Lyman Allyn Art Museum, New London, Conn.)

The freshman girls of the Manual Training and Industrial School, later Chapman Technical High School, learn to cook in a "domestic science laboratory" on October 19, 1909. The school on Waller Street opened in 1906 and taught practical trades to boys and girls. (Public Library of New London.)

For boys, a practical trade was more likely to be something like the machine tool laboratory seen here in January 1910. Chapman Tech existed until 1951, when it merged with Bulkeley School to form New London High School. (Public Library of New London.)

This class at Nathan Hale Grammar School from around 1907 was gender-segregated. All the girls are at left, and the boys are at right. As they grew older, the segregation continued, with boys and girls going to different high schools. (Courtesy New London County Historical Society.)

Bulkeley was the high school for boys, and girls attended Williams Memorial Institute on Broad Street, which replaced an older girls' school in 1891. Harriet Peck Williams left a trust fund to establish the free girls' school as a memorial to her son, Thomas W. Williams II. This is the Class of 1907. (Public Library of New London.)

Judges and lawyers of New London gathered for a portrait around 1910. The portrait hanging at left is that of Augustus Brandegee, a judge, legislator, mayor of New London, and speaker of the Connecticut House of Representatives. (Public Library of New London.)

New London Business College was founded in 1887 by Robert A. Brubeck. This photograph was taken outside the school's State Street home around 1904. The school, which produces secretaries, accountants, and office assistants, has survived several changes of name and ownership and today is a branch of the Ridley Lowell Business and Technical Institute. (Courtesy New London County Historical Society.)

Eight

A Late Tour of the City

Buildings and yards once went right up to the railroad tracks behind Bank Street where South Water Street now runs. At left is the U.S. Custom House. Most of the other structures are long gone. (New London Landmarks.)

This photograph and those at the top of the next five pages give a nearly 360-degree view of downtown New London from the top of the Mohican Hotel at the turn of the century. This view is looking due east down State Street, with the First Congregational Church in the foreground. (Public Library of New London.)

The turn-of-the-century waterfront was typically lined with steamboats like the *City of Worcester* (left) and freight vessels like the *Mohawk* and *Mohegan* (right), which belonged to the

Looking southeast from the Mohican, Fort Trumbull is in the far distance, and the railroad bridge over Shaw's Cove is at right. This photograph was taken over the roof of the Palmer Brothers Co. on Washington Street, where bed quilts were made. (Public Library of New London.)

Central Vermont Railway. Note the Mohican Hotel, which still had only eight of its eleven stories. (Richard Gipstein.)

This view southwest from the Mohican takes in the Huntington Street Baptist Church (at left) and nearby houses. The building at lower right housed the boys' and girls' room of the Public Library of New London. (Public Library of New London.)

Looking up Broad Street from Huntington, the Mount Vernon House was the most striking feature of the landscape. Built around 1796 by Gen. Jedidiah Hungtington, a veteran of the American Revolution and friend of George Washington, it was modeled and named after

The courthouse on Huntington Street is seen here looking west from the Mohican. Before it stands the Liberty Pole. The landmark flagpole had been moved from the Parade after the Soldiers and Sailors Monument was erected. At lower right is the Williams Mansion, where the Garde Arts Center now stands. (Public Library of New London.)

Washington's home in Virginia. In the 1940s it was razed to make way for an A&P supermarket. (Public Library of New London.)

Another shot from the Mohican, looking north, shows Meridian Street at left. At far left is St. James Episcopal Church. The twin-spired building at right is the old Federal Street Methodist Church, which stood where the rear parking lot of the Radisson Hotel is. (Public Library of New London.)

The Parade is captured in this panoramic view around 1908. The Soldiers and Sailors Monument dominates the scene, and a parklet, complete with cannons, has been added behind it. There is still a small watering trough for horses, though the automobile would soon make it

This final view from atop the Mohican, looking northeast, shows the old railroad bridge over the Thames River. In the foreground is the main plant of the Brainerd and Armstrong Co. at Church and Union Streets. (Public Library of New London.)

obsolete. The Neptune Building (center right) has replaced the Old Yellow Building. (Public Library of New London.)

Four young women (at right) chat on the steps of the old post office at State and Union Streets around the turn of the century. Beyond is the Crocker House, showing an ornate top floor later destroyed in a fire. At left is the Harris Building, the home of Hislop's department store. (Courtesy New London County Historical Society.)

Electrical wires on State Street were the only hint of the future as late as the 1890s, when the horse and carriage was still the most popular way to get around. But that had already begun to change, as shown by the new trolley tracks curving onto Main Street. At far left there is only empty space where the Mohican Hotel would soon stand. (Connecticut Historical Society, Hartford, Conn.)

The Old Yellow Building was about to vanish when this photograph was taken in early 1898. Signs are advertising a going-out-of-business sale at the Brown Paint Co., the building's last tenant. The Parade landmark was razed to make way for the Neptune Building. The other placards are for an upcoming engagement by Payton's Big Comedy Co. ("Nothing Cheap But the Prices") at the Lyceum Theatre. (Public Library of New London.)

A steamroller paves Bank Street at Tilley on January 8, 1892. In the background is the Keefe House, built around 1740 by Capt. Joseph Coit, whose shipyard lay directly opposite. The building was razed in 1924. (Public Library of New London.)

Three young women pose on the cobblestones at Bank and Reed Streets, near where the statue of Christopher Columbus was later erected. The Dart Building at right went up in 1892 and still stands. It has been the longtime home of Carlo's, an Italian restaurant.

The area where Reed, Blinman, Howard, and Bank Streets meet was seen as a hindrance to traffic. In 1920 the city bought the plot, demolished the buildings, created a small park, and widened the streets. Once known as Tyler Square, the area is now the site of the Christopher Columbus statue.

Workmen gather around a fountain at Bank and Truman Streets in the late nineteenth century in this photograph taken by Edward Cook. At right, houses line the south side of Bank Street. The area was left empty by urban renewal in the 1960s.

The Ramrod Schoolhouse was once the oldest surviving school building in New London and was believed to have been built in the late eighteenth century. Three generations of children attended the school, where the desks were sawed from the trunk of an oak tree, with the branches used as legs. The building stood at Bank and Hobron Streets, the area later turned into Garibaldi Park. (Public Library of New London.)

The Lyceum Theatre on Washington Street opened in 1890 and during its heyday was host to giants such as actress Sarah Bernhardt and violinist Fritz Kreisler. In 1901 a memorial service for assassinated President William McKinley was held here. Doomed by the popularity of movies, the theater closed in 1932, and the building was razed in 1959. (Public Library of New London.)

The State Armory at Coit and Washington Streets was built in 1884 on the site of the Alfred Coit home and was headquarters to the National Guard's 3rd Regiment and later the 192nd Field Artillery. It was demolished in 1962 as part of the city's Redevelopment program. (Public Library of New London.)

The old St. James Episcopal Church at Main and Church Streets was built in 1785–87 for Samuel Seabury, the first Episcopal bishop in America. After the church moved in 1850, the building was used by the Universalists and later was known as Avery's Stable. This view from about 1900 shows a second-floor porch that had been added. The building burned in 1919. (Public Library of New London.)

Memorial Hospital, the first such institution in the city, opened in 1893 after merchant and politician Jonathan N. Harris gave $10,000 for its founding. This building at Jefferson and Garfield Avenues was its home until 1918 when, for want of a more modern facility, Memorial Hospital merged with the Joseph Lawrence Free Public Hospital. (Public Library of New London.)

Two bloomer-clad bicyclists glide down Broad Street near the Second Congregational Church in this peaceful turn-of-the-century scene. Except for the trees and trolley tracks, not much has changed. The house at center right, one in from Brainard Street, was the home of William H. Rowe, cashier of the New London City National Bank.

Riverside Park on the Thames River seems far away from the city in this idyllic *c.* 1910 view. Part of the property was donated to the city as an incentive to buy Ocean Beach in the late nineteenth century. The rest was donated by whaling scion Sebastian D. Lawrence, judge and politician Augustus Brandegee, and industrialist George S. Palmer. (Public Library of New London.)

After the city's street layout was rearranged during Redevelopment, this corner, Main and Federal Streets, ceased to exist. The streets no longer intersect. The houses in the foreground were just north of where the police station is now. The only thing there today is a guardrail. (New London Landmarks.)

This view northeast from the First Congregational Church shows the section of the city hardest hit by Redevelopment. Almost everything in the picture is gone. At lower left is a dormer of the Brainerd and Armstrong Co., and below it, the corner of Church and Union Streets. (Public Library of New London.)

Church Street was once a narrow lane bordered by a stone wall. Today, as Governor Winthrop Boulevard, the street is much wider. At left is the courthouse, and at center is the home of banker Walter Learned. The site was later a Methodist church and today is the courthouse annex. (Public Library of New London.)

Williams Street at Manwaring looked like this around 1896. The parklet at right is known for an 1871 howitzer that has been there for years. During the attack by Benedict Arnold, residents fired on the advancing British with a cannon from this spot. Three or four British casualties are buried nearby. (Courtesy New London County Historical Society.)

The Dimock house on Twelfth Street in East New London was uprooted to make way for State Pier. Loaded onto a barge, it was hauled down the Thames by tug on June 1, 1914, to a new location. At right is the building on Water Street that had housed C.D. Boss and Son. The cracker business had folded two years earlier. (Lyman Allyn Art Museum, New London, Conn.)

Acknowledgments

Thanks are due to the following institutions and individuals, who allowed me to borrow or copy the more than two hundred photographs in this book or who assisted me in my research:

Mary Beth Baker of the Antiquarian and Landmarks Society; Phil Budlong, associate curator at Mystic Seaport Museum; Jacklyn Burns of the J. Paul Getty Museum; Carey Congdon; David J. Corrigan, curator of the Museum of Connecticut History; Chris Curran of Citizens Bank; Richard Gipstein; Tom Hahn; Marjorie Ealahan Heap; Toni Hulse, assistant curator of the Lyman Allyn Art Museum; Dr. Mark Jones, the Connecticut state archivist; Carol Kimball; Brian McCarthy; Kathryn Miller of the Public Library of New London; Stephanie Morton of New London Landmarks; William Peterson, curator of the Mystic Seaport Museum; my colleague Michael Remus at *The Day*; Stephen Rice, curator of graphics at the Connecticut Historical Society; Sally Ryan of New London Landmarks; and Alma Wies.

I am especially grateful to Alice Sheriff, director and curator of the New London County Historical Society, for her relentless and cheerful assistance and for the privileged status she has accorded me on this and many other occasions.

Bibliography

Baker, Mary Beth. "General Description: The Hempsted Houses."

Caulkins, Frances Manwaring. *History of New London, Connecticut from the First Survey of the Coast in 1612, to 1860.* H.D. Utley, New London, Conn., 1895.

Churchill, Sharon P. "The Pequot Colony." *Tidings* Magazine, September-October 1987.

Colby, Barnard L. *For Oil and Buggy Whips: Whaling Captains of New London County, Connecticut.* Mystic Seaport Museum Inc., Mystic, Conn., 1990.

Daily Star, The.

Day, The.

Decker, Robert Owen. *The Whaling City: A History of New London.* The Pequot Press, Chester, Conn., 1976.

Decker, Robert Owen. *Whaling Industry of New London.* Liberty Cap Books, York, Pa., 1973.

Dictionary of American Naval Fighting Ships. Navy Department, 1959.

Hamilton, Harlan. *Lights & Legends: A Historical Guide to Lighthouses of Long Island Sound, Fishers Island Sound and Block Island Sound.* Wescott Cove Publishing Co., Stamford, Conn., 1987.

Leading Business Merchants of New London and Vicinity Embracing Groton and Niantic, Mercantile Publishing Co., 1890.

Manke, Rita and Robert. "Mr. Lawrence's Fireman's Monument." 1984.

New London Evening Telegram.

Noyes, Gertrude E. *The Savings Bank of New London at 150: 1827–1977.*

Picturesque New London and Its Environs. The American Book Exchange, Hartford, Conn., 1901.

Starr, W.H. *A Centennial Historical Sketch of the Town of New London.* 1876.

Turner, Gregg M. and Melancthon W. Jacobus. *Connecticut Railroads: An Illustrated History.* The Connecticut Historical Society, 1989.

Wall, Richard B. Various historical articles in *The Day*.

Wood, Frederic J. *The Turnpikes of New England.* Branch Line Press, Pepperell, Mass., 1997.